RITUALS OF THE IMAGINATION

Rituals of the Imagination

Thomas Moore

With a New Preface by the Author

The Dallas Institute Publications
Dallas

Cover: design by Intentions Graphic Design
photo by Paul Loven

ISBN 0-911005-03-X

The Dallas Institute Publications, formerly known as The Pegasus Foundation,
publishes works concerned with the imaginative, mythic, and symbolic sources of
culture. Publication efforts are centered at:

The Dallas Institute of Humanities and Culture
2719 Routh Street, Dallas, Texas 75201
214.871.2440
www.dallasinstitute.org

New Preface by the Author

Writing books is an odd experience. I would have thought that almost twenty years after a book was written, for the author, at least, it would be out of date and stale. But I find that the essays in this little volume stay with me, fresh and fruitful. I keep returning in my current thinking and writing to the ideas I expressed here about ritual, especially the derivations of the word and the connection between neurotic rituals and religious ones. Often I want to restate, and in fact sometimes do, the ideas about the color green, especially on football fields and billiard tables. This image still helps me appreciate the role of play and sport in giving the soul a place to be exercised in a largely ego-driven society. I keep thinking about myth and writing about it. Myth still remains hidden under a layer of unconsciousness in the stories told in popular culture today. And finally, I am amazed how enduring my work on Marsilio Ficino has been for me. Over and over I find myself writing in my books, "Ficino says. . . ."

This book of essays represents a period in my life that becomes more and more precious to me as time goes by. I learned many things at the Dallas Institute of Humanities and Culture in the early 1980's: the basics of a method for archetypal psychology, the role of mythological thinking in relation to culture in general and cities in particular, and the place of literature, classical and otherwise, in a continuing education. I also witnessed how a group of honest thinkers can influence people in many different professions to think more deeply and more imaginatively.

When these lectures were delivered, many of us present thought that archetypal psychology might one day become a movement and have some recognition in the society at large. But what has happened couldn't have been predicted. Better than a movement, which easily calcifies into a system, we have seen each of the men and women who were leaders in Dallas become more individual as they pursue their own imaginations. The result is a living thing, rather than a dead organization. We have also seen the Dallas Institute change, grow, and be vital.

The shadow side of this flourishing of individuals is the professional and academic worlds' failure to see sufficiently the value of the work of James Hillman, Patricia Berry, Robert Sardello, and others who were in the 1980's community. The imagination still plays second fiddle to highly abstract rationality, quantification, and practicality–avenues of thought that dominate the writings of specialists and seep into the popular culture. The imagination is not rigorous enough to many academics. I still find the word "rigor" being used to separate imagination from these other methods and associate it with *rigor mortis*.

Personally, I'm rather mystified about what has happened to me since giving these lectures. I continue to write about things that interest me, often odd things looked at from an odd point of view. Recently I was writing about the Lapis Lazuli Radiant Buddha of Healing–color still intrigues me. Yet the popular media treats me as though I were a "spiritual" writer–no one seems to distinguish soul from spirit–or a self-help guide. I hope there is more playfulness, irony, and depth in what I am doing than is usual in these genres, but maybe not. I have found that writing books that are read in great numbers has a sobering effect on my writing process. Perhaps the puer has been tamed a little.

The exercise of a deep imagination is a sign that a group or a culture still has a heart and soul. As I try to keep up with developments in the arts and culture, I don't see many creative people sticking their heads outside the sphere of conventional thought. I don't see many looking through the chinks in the cosmic egg of our agreed upon worldview. I don't see much influence of the arts, spirituality, or academia on the severe problems of our world at home and abroad. The Dallas Institute has offered a brilliant model of a group of intellectuals supporting each other and at the same time able to influence their own society. If we can't achieve this on a larger scale, I don't see how we can avoid making the twenty-first century more psychotically bloody than the twentieth. It all depends on the depth and relevance of our work in imagination. I don't worry about relevance or popularity contaminating my work, but at the same time I want to preserve the depth and the poetical approach.

One final point: I trust the work of small groups more than that of large movements. Small is indeed beautiful, and local is smart. A little book draws considerable power from a small group with a big imagination and a great heart. I am grateful beyond words to the Institute for initially supporting a neophyte lecturer and writer and for keeping his book in print. I am especially grateful to Dr. Robert Sardello for inviting me to do this book in the first place and to Dr. Gail Thomas and Dr. Joanne Stroud for making it happen and for giving me years of invaluable friendship and counsel.

Thomas Moore

A *former professor of religion and psychology, Thomas Moore is the best selling author of* Care of the Soul, Soul Mates, *and* Re-Enchantment of Everyday Life. *In his writing, Moore uses the language of the world's religions to find insight into daily human life. He uses words like mystery, magic, eros, and of course, soul to preserve the complexity of life even as he advocates a return to the ordinary and simple. In his latest book,* Original Self, *due for release in March 2000, Moore offers illuminating meditations on living with passion and originality.*

Ritual: A Moving Act of Imagination

> ... riverrun, past Eve and Adam's,
> from swerve of shore to bend of bay,
> brings us by a commodius vicus of
> recirculation back to Howth Castle
> and Environs.
>   Sir Tristram, violer d'amores, fr'over
> the the short sea, had passencore rear-
> rived from North Amrorica on this
> side the scraggy isthmus of Europe
> Minor to wielder fight his penisolate
> war:
>
> James Joyce, *Finnegan's Wake*

THE WORD "RITUAL" is from Latin *ritus*, from Greek *rheo*, meaning "to flow, run, rush, or stream." A "rite" is a river—*rivus*—"river or stream"; related to "rival," one who uses the same stream as another. One *ar*rives, or, as in this case, *de*rives, by approaching or leading from the river.

To be in ritual, therefore, is to be in the river: Jesus with John the Baptist, the Buddhist on his raft in the river. Using the word from which "ritual" derives, Herakleitos says:

> Everything flows and nothing abides; everything
> gives way and nothing stays fixed.
>
> (Wheelwright, fr. 20)

Everything flows: *panta rhei*. And again Herakleitos, in a familiar phrase: "You cannot step twice into the same river, for other waters are continually flowing on" (*epirrei*: "flowing on").

To be in ritual is to be in the river. One does not find baptism at the river; rather, one finds the river in baptism. It is the river one is searching for.

To be in ritual is to be in Joyce's river, flowing in a Viconian circle or cycle that includes Eve and Adam's place, the rivers of Paradise and of the Parents, and that continually flowing stream where they can say: Here Comes Everybody. Here Comes Everybody: not common human destiny and not a collective unconscious, but every current and figure contacted and conjured in ritual.

The eighth chapter of the *Tao Te Ching* begins:

> The highest good is like water.
> Water gives life to the ten thousand things
>   and does not strive.
> It flows in places men reject
>   and so it is like the Tao.

To be in ritual is to be in a stream like the water of the Tao. The Tao—the ways things go. To strive against the Tao is to force water higher than the level it seeks. In the flowing water one does not strive, one does not need to strive. The River is the Tao, the

Law, the way things are as distinct from the way we think things ought to be.

Tristan, repeatedly wounded after flashes of heroism, sought the sea, moved by an eros for another shore. Violer d'amores, Joyce calls him, musician and lover in the same phrase, Orpheus-like in his musical style, Hermetic in his way of moving and talking, floating rudderless on the water, not striving, not directing. Tristan is in ritual when he is on the sea to Ireland, to Joyce's Liffey (Campbell), the river of Ulysses, who is himself like a river, taking many turns (polytropos), like Finn again. In Joyce's myth, to be in ritual is to be on the river Liffey, to be the incarnation of Finn McCool, or to be out of one's striving and in the myth, in the river, at sea, adrift, like Tristan armed and provisioned only with music, with the lyre, the seven strings of the musical scale, the seven planetary tones, the aesthetic and imaginative dealing with destiny. Here Comes Everybody, Joyce intones repeatedly. In ritual: Here Comes Everybody.

Ritual is like myth in many respects. There is a difference between living a myth and telling a myth, between mythic sensibility and a knowledge of mythology, between comparing one's life to myth and seeing one's life through myth or as myth. In a similar way, there is a difference between enacting a ritual and acting ritually, between formal ritual and ritual sensibility, between ritual times or places and times or places as ritual, between a love of ritual and a ritual sense.

To be in ritual is to be like Tristan, rudderless, without a steering ego, but equipped with a musical instrument, an imagining ego. Tristan is clever. He knows many languages. He uses his musical talent to *arrive*, that is, to stream, to high places. To be in ritual is not simply to be adrift, but to be adrift with an instrument that is not a rudder. A ritual sense gives life to the ten thousand things, to multiplicity unimaginable.

Lao Tze goes further. Water flows in places people reject, and so it is like the Tao. You can refuse and strive against the current, against your destiny, against the stirring of your daimon. Not to be in ritual is to strive, perhaps to run aground, shipwrecked, stuck. Neurosis and psychosis: being without a ritual sense.

But we all know that psychotics are highly ritualistic, that churchgoers are as stuck as anybody.

There is a law of the psyche—this is the way things seem to go. What you require, you do not see, or fear, or struggle against. What you require tends to be *diverted* into a monstrosity or caricature of itself. You require myth, and yet you grasp at *a* mythology. You require a ritual way of acting, and you grab onto ritualism. The psychotic, having lost the Tao, separated from his own stream, ignorant of the Law of his own life, becomes fascinated with minor laws, caricatures of the real thing. When a flowing, imaginative style is thwarted by heroics and protectiveness, for whatever reason, images stream in as diversions. When single-eyed sincerity urges a person to find *the* proper, truthful stream, in a religion, for example, or in *EST*, his religious sense is diverted and blocked.

Tristan, too, occasionally exchanges his musical instrument for a sword. He turns hero and slays the dragon on his way to Isolde. Knightly and militant, he prevails over the beast of imagination; but then he is overcome, stupified, by the dragon's tongue. The voice of imagination makes the hero go prostrate, flattened, flaccid on his penisolate quest. Imagination gone monstrous. Psychotic ritualism is the dragon's tongue laying low the heroic longing.

Ritual that moves the psyche is intimately connected to ritualism that makes it stuck, that renders attention self-conscious, absorbed in an absurdly selective, focused object, like the steps we take when walking or the navel we gaze at. Erik Erikson disagrees. Psychological ritual is entirely different, he says, from the rituals found in anthropology "from which all participants emerge with a sense of awe and purification" (*Toys and Reasons*, p. 78).

The problem is, both awesome ritualism and painful psychotic ritualism are *tremendum et fascinans*. The man who can't step on a crack lest he break his mother's back, or must step on that line, feels the awe and wrath of heaven and hell. At all costs he must step on that line or avoid that crack. But nothing flows in these kinds of ritual: time stops, the river dries up, the only thing that exists is that line which must be stepped upon. The penalties are severe: purgatory without indulgence, hell without respite. This is Sisyphus rolling his rock to no purpose, repeatedly, defeatedly. Camus says this is absurd; that is, literally, without any sound or tone of meaning—no lyre, no musical notes, nothing Orphic, nothing Hermetic. Psychotic ritual moves nothing and is not moving.

A way out, a tonic for ritualism, might be homeopathy. A deepened ritual sense might deal with formalistic and psychotic ritual. Tristan, after his heroic effort, returns to the water, to a bathtub or to the sea, like Jesus with John: a Viconian *commodius* circuit, from the hero to the Gods. Those stuck in ritual, in the church or in the ward, do not need to *do* anything. They need a ritual sense, homeopathically, a ritualizing of everything and of the everyday to get the water flowing, to get into the river, to be baptized, renewed, like Jesus, like Tristan. The caricature is to be a reborn Christian rather than like Jesus reborn.

If I want to step into the river flowing through the concrete structures of my life, I may, for example, *confess*. I may confess ritually, actually saying, within my everyday world but not to it, "I confess." I confess that sometimes I'm like a child. I confess that this situation frightens me. Then my words are not expression, and they are not communication to anybody. In this world they do nothing. But, by a Viconian *commodius vicus* of recirculation they work wonders. In religion one says: I confess to Almighty God, to Blessed Mary ever Virgin, to Blessed Michael the Archangel, to Blessed John the Baptist" (whom we've met before) "to the Holy Apostles Peter and Paul, and to all the saints. . . ." In ritual you do not confess to anybody, not even to yourself, but to the God, to your virginal soul, to your angelic nature, to your own baptist in the river, to your inner persons, Peter, Paul, or whomever they are. The psychotic knows that these are the ones who demand the confession and are the only ones who can give absolution and ease of mind.

Or, in ritual you sacrifice. That is to say, you make the most valuable, prized things in life sacred, set aside for the Gods, not available for ordinary human commerce, not understood in ordinary human terms. A commentary on the Hindu Vedic sacrifice says:

> The Gods know not to neglect it (sacrifice) because "it is their principle of life." "It is their nourishment." The Gods subsist from that which one offers them here (on earth) as men subsist from gifts which come to them from the celestial world." "The sacrifice is the vehicle which brings the Gods."
>
> (Sylvain Levi, p. 5)

By sacrificing *expression* and making it *confession*, you sacrifice the attachment, the human interchange, along with human solutions and aid, to the Gods, to Peter and Paul. To confess to one of these, even in human conversation, but for the benefit of the Gods, is to bring the Gods into the scene. The one to whom you address words is imaginary and imaginal, and your words are like the songs of Tristan who floated in the sea, trusting, full of faith, that his music would get him to Dublin, and to the love of his soul, Isolde.

Words can be ritualized acts, if they are put in the river, in the stream of imagination. Perhaps the most common ritual words are the obscene ones, "obscene"—literally, "off the stage, out of the scene," not in the logic of the action. They do nothing in the way words usually do.

Ferenczi wrote a splendid essay on obscene words in which he says:

> An obscene word has a peculiar power of compelling the hearer to imagine the object it denotes, the sexual organ or function, in substantial actuality. . . . *Freud, on investigating the psychogenesis of the pleasure afforded by wit, recognized the significance of child's play with words. "Children," he says, "treat words as objects."* (139–140)

Ferenczi adds: "We come to the conclusion that obscene words have attributes which all words must have possessed in some early stage of psychical development" (138). We might add that all words might still possess that ritual capacity. Words can make us imagine the object, words themselves can be treated as objects. These are words thrown into the river. "This is my body"—a river phrase at times. "I confess"—a word to Peter and Paul.

According to Herakleitos, we cannot step twice into this river of ritual. It is never the same. Only outside of ritual, in daily commerce, can we hold a person to his word and to his meaning. *Finnegan's Wake* is a ritualizing of language, Joyce the transubstantiating priest. The stream of consciousness often attributed to Joyce is rather the ritual quality of his language in which the reader is invited to bathe.

Dialogue with a Doubter

Why is religious ritual awesome and somber, while psychotic ritual is often funny? In the film Being There, *Chauncey Gardner has just spoken to the president and is told he has a call from the financial editor of a major newspaper. He starts walking toward the phone in a fancy office. But on his way, he plays a little hop-scotch with the lines of the floor. The audience laughs. Why?*

Good question, but I'm not sure I can give you a satisfying answer. Laughter tears apart our pretensions, our serious surface world. Perhaps the Gods speak more directly through psychotic behavior, showing us the flatness of our serious business.

What about the first part of the question—religion? You've avoided that.

I was hoping to avoid some trouble. We laugh at psychotic ritual because it has no connection with the ordinary, serious world. We are unnaturally somber in religious ritual for much the same reason. The poles of sobriety and hilarity only serve to put the two forms of ritualism, neither of which move, in the same boat. Maybe if someone would rock the boat, they'd end up in the river.

Does this have anything to do with the absurd?

Funny you should ask. I was going to quote from Samuel Beckett who displays the funny side of the absurd. Here is his very ritualized description of a fellow named Watt:

Watt's way of advancing due east, for example, was to turn his bust as far as possible towards the north and at the same time to fling out his right leg as far as possible towards the south, and then to turn his bust as far as possible towards the south and at the same time to fling out his left leg as far as possible towards the north, and then again to turn his bust as far as possible towards the north and to fling out his right leg as far as possible towards the south, and then again to turn his bust as far as possible toward the south and to fling out his left leg as far as possible toward the north, and so on, over and over again, many many times, until he reached his destination, and could sit down. So, standing first on one leg, and then on the other, he moved forward, a headlong tardigrade, in a straight line. The knees, on these occasions, did not bend. They could have, but they did not. No knees could better bend than Watt's, when they chose, there was nothing the matter with Watt's knees, as may appear. But when out walking they did not bend, for some obscure reason. Notwithstanding this, the feet fell, heel and sole together, flat upon the ground and left it, for the air's uncharted ways, with manifest repugnancy. The arms were content to dangle, in perfect equipendency. (Watt, 30)

What was that all about? And why does Beckett repeat himself so much?

Ritual is repetitive. Beckett's words do what they say. He shows us a picture of the human being in the absurdity of his ritualism.

But why would such a sad picture be so funny?

Because ritualism turns people into things. Instead of seeing the world, through ritual, as an object of fantasy, we become the objects in ritualism. This is not a description of a who, but of a What, a Watt.

And Beckett won a Nobel Prize in literature for this?

Yes, because an accurate, bold view of diversionary rituals is a step toward a sense of ritual. Besides, if you think of it, Watt isn't so different from those long-legged, kneeless figures of Giacometti, is he?

I prefer something more noble.

Well, religion gives you the noble side, and some art can do so as well. Jean Genet, whose drama is like ritual sometimes, thinks that Giacometti's figures are the best example of ritual in art. Personality is taken from them, like actors with masks. They often appear in groups—repetition without individuality.

Isn't theater essentially ritual?

No, wrong again. Theater may be ritual-like when it drops the illusion of daily life, its naturalism, and when it strips down to inner structures, like Giacometti. But theater is not ritual because it is watched, only seen. Ritual is not a spectator activity. Ritual is observed in theater.

End of Dialogue

The question about theater and ritual is a good one. Both have stage directions and a script. In ritual, the script is a text of carefully thought-out words or at least words that don't mean only what they seem to mean. The words are objects, not direct expressions. When a person has a habit (itself a diversionary ritual) of saying: "I'm no expert, but . . ." and then goes on to tell you what he thinks, authoritatively, you might do well to hear those words as a ritual rather than as plain expression.

Ritual also has stage directions, or in the language of religion, *rubrics*—the words printed in red, not to be spoken but to be followed. Rubrics indicate a will other than the person acting. A psychotic knows what he has to do, perhaps hang blue flowers in every other window in this room, whisper certain words rather than speaking out loud, or tap his knee for several minutes. Rubrics imply another will, another law. The question is, however, is it the will of a daimon or a tormentor?

Psychotherapy can be ritual. Not simply because one meets regularly, at the same time and place weekly, in a formal situation. Therapy is ritual when the persons involved are off the dry land of reasons and events and in the stream of fantasies. Moreover, therapy is ritual when one sails like Tristan in the fantasies brought to therapy. Therapy is ritual when one takes his rubrics from the dream or the fantasies embedded in a problem or in the unselfconscious language that arises in therapy.

Sex, they say, is ritual. But not as habit, of course. The caricatures of ritual: habit, formalism, lack of involvement, regularity, repetition, and obsession—these only point to a loss of the ritual sense. Sex is ritual more in the sense that the rubrics are not personal and conscious, and when there is nothing to be done or accomplished—the Tristan complex in sex. Freud says, quite accurately, that obsessive ritualism is a manifestation of the repression of sex.

Theologians also have something to say about the nonego aspects of ritual. Ritual, they say officially, works not *ex opere operantis*, that is, literally, from the work of the one doing the ritual, but *ex opera operato*, that is, from the work that is done. In theology, it makes no difference what the moral character or the intention of the priest might be. The ritual is effective in spite of these intentions and character. The essence of ritual is to be beyond intention and beyond personality. This is a point of doctrine, and of psychology, that is easily misunderstood and readily falls into caricature. Ritual becomes automatism. W. H. Auden in his poem "Profile" says:

> So obsessive a ritualist
> a pleasant surprise
> makes him cross.

The point in ritual is to give up intention, the intentional fallacy applied to life. Inherent in ritual is such a sacrifice of will. Again, further on in his poem, Auden makes this point:

> In anxiety dreams
> at the moment he gives up hope
> he ejaculates.

This is a Tristan image. Eros is fulfilled at the moment of surrender to another rubric. The telos of ritualistic acts, whether psychotic, neurotic, or religious, is the recovery of the Tao, but these acts are not it. The Tao is the flowing water that makes Jesus the Christ, Siddhartha the Buddha, and perhaps Watt Who. Moving ritual might loosen Watt's knees and maybe even Giacometti's. It might loosen the demands for obsessive rubrics and get repetitious acts, interpretations, and reasons moving again.

Perhaps one of the reasons we are so often caught in diversionary rituals is that we don't love our own Law, the Tao as it is in us. We have affection for law and order, for customs and traditions, for familiar ways of thinking and acting, but we don't love the Law that flows within, our own river. Fortunately we sometimes do find our way back to the banks of this river, in a book, a person, a poem, a metaphor, or a minute of music. Here is the way Herman Hesse describes this discovery in his novel, *Siddhartha:*

> As he went on speaking and Vasudeva listened to him with a serene face, Siddhartha was more keenly aware than ever of Vasudeva's attentiveness. He felt his troubles, his anxieties and his secret hopes flow across to him and then return again. Disclosing his wound to this listener was the same as bathing it in the river, until it became cool and one with the river. As he went on talking and confessing, Siddhartha felt more and more that this was no longer Vasudeva, no longer a man who was listening to him. He felt that this motionless listener was absorbing his confession as a tree absorbs the rain, that this motionless man was the river itself, that he was God Himself, that he was eternity itself. As Siddhartha stopped thinking about himself and his wound, this recognition of the change in Vasudeva possessed him, and the more he realized it, the less strange did he find it; the more did he realize that everything was natural and in order, that Vasudeva had long ago, almost always been like that, only he did not quite recognize it; indeed he himself was hardly different from him.

Given as we are to placing value on reflection and on imagination and to knowing the problems of heroism, we may wonder sometimes how to act. In therapy a person finds himself saying over and over: there is nothing to be done, no resolutions to make, no progress to chart, no past to overcome, no promise to fulfill, no right attitude to achieve. These all tend toward heroism and hyperactivity and ultimately to more anxiety. There is nothing to do but there is plenty of action to take place. A ritual sense, a Tristan complex which has a love for the music of action, an attention to the nonhuman rubrics that, in red, are easily overlooked—these provide the kind of foundation that action can have: not solid earth, but a flowing river.

References

Campbell, Joseph. *The Masks of God: Creative Mythology.* New York: The Viking Press, 1968.

Erickson, Erik. *Toys and Reasons: Stages in the Ritualization of Experience.* New York: W.W. Norton, 1977.

Ferenczi, Sandor. "On Obscene Words." *First Contributions to Psychoanalysis.* Translated by Ernest Jones. New York: Brunner/Mazel, 1952.

Levi, Sylvain. *La Doctrine du sacrifice dans les Bráhmanas.* 2nd ed. Bibliothéque de l'Ecole des Hautes Etudes, Sciences Religieuses 73. Paris, 1966.

Is the Personal Myth a Myth?

THE IDEA OF a personal myth appears, among other places, in the prologue to C. G. Jung's *Memories, Dreams, Reflections*:

> *Thus it is that I have now undertaken, in my eighty-third year, to tell my personal myth. I can only make direct statements, only "tell stories." Whether or not the stories are "true" is not the problem. The only question is whether what I tell is my fable, my truth.*

In these few lines we have not only the idea of a personal myth but also several puzzles associated with that idea. How, for example, can you tell the story of your life and not be concerned whether it is true or not? Jung seems to equate the personal myth with telling stories, but is there a difference between your own story and your personal myth? And how can we, many of us suspicious of personalism, appreciate Jung's wish to tell *his* fable and *his* truth?

With all of these questions in mind, it is not surprising that the title of this essay is a question, and a question that can be asked in many ways. Is the personal myth a myth? On one level I'm asking: Is there such a thing as a personal myth, or is the whole idea a myth, an illusion? Or, in another sense, is the personal myth a genuine myth, or is the word "myth" in that phrase only a remote metaphor? Finally, a more contorted sense of the question: What is the myth behind the notion of a personal myth? What are the mythic roots of the idea of a personal myth? Is the personal myth *a* myth?

To engage these questions, let me go back to basics and say something about the nature of myth itself. First, I think we myth specialists should stop complaining about the popular understanding of myth: that it is something that is not true. Myth *is* not true. I would say that myth doesn't even convey truth. Myth merely offers a way of imagining events, events either out there in the world or events not out there in the world. The Greek word *mythos* consistently refers to story and fable. It is contrasted with *logos*, which is the hound of truth. Myth has for its scope and range mere imagination, pure imagination.

Liddell and Scott, in their Greek lexicon, make some surprising remarks about myth. They say, for instance, that *mythos* is used of *a story that never comes to an end.* But how can there be a story that has no end? It just goes on forever? If it doesn't have an end, it can't very well have a middle. You wonder if it can even have a beginning. In fact, it isn't easy to find the beginning of a mythic story. Earlier stories and other mythic figures so often seem implicated in the myth you are trying to understand. It is also difficult to find the original version of a mythic story, to trace its own beginnings. Stories of myth also seem to be literally *open-ended,* that is, they never end but always give way to new versions and fresh interpretations. Maybe a myth is better imagined as a kaleidoscope of images, so that the mythic fragment of Oedipus we find in Freud is part of the myth, even if Freud's Oedipus seems to have been plucked out of his Sophoclean setting. Perhaps those figures of Jewish and Christian myth carved in stone that sit perched on European cathedrals are true versions of myth—eternal, fragmented, not framed with a beginning and end, generative, animating, suggestive of story but not at the moment in a story.

If we persist in considering myth as a story, we still have trouble holding it together. There are the countless versions of myth. Is Aphrodite the mother of Eros? Or is Eros, as in Hesiod and in the Orphic hymn, one of the first and primary gods? Is Artemis the lady of beasts, a mother, a virgin, a moon goddess? Sometimes she is these things, sometimes she isn't. As myth travels through time it seems as loose as a cheap necklace, broken apart here and there and pasted together haphazardly. Maybe we should stop treating these holes and contradictions in myth as anomalies and see them as being of the essence of myth. Later, when entertaining the idea of a personal myth, we should keep in mind this tendency of myth toward fragmentation, this nonlinear, loose, unending, broken quality of myth.

The other startling comment on myth we find in Liddell and Scott is this: *myth is a story told to those who do not listen.* This reminds me of the music Erik Satie used to write, intending it to be performed on stage between acts of a play when the audience was out in the lobby enjoying a smoke. Who would tell a story to someone who would not listen? But there is, in fact, something suicidal, something self-destructive, about myth. Myth wants to be told and then destroyed. It wants to be heard but not listened to. The most dangerous, dark side of myth is that it is often a story heard and then not forgotten. It is quite important to forget a story, especially one that carries the weight and authority usually given to myth. The same is true, by the way, of stories told in therapy or in analysis. The patient might hope to remember all the insights and truth-bearing stories that come up in therapy, but such a literal memory would be an obstacle. It would reduce memory to the storage of information. It is best to forget these stories and let them fragment, disintegrate, and in fragmentation become specks in the fabric of your own tradition, the personal myth. In culture, the truly beautiful remains of myth we enjoy today are not only the stories but also the fragments painted on vases and carved on cathedrals: Perseus frozen in his flight from Medusa; Jesus in the middle of a sentence on the mountain, and personally, an instant from a memory flashed in a dream.

Myth is not a story. Myth is the discrete, personified, geographical, differentiated world, full of animals and gods, maintained by story and by art. The personal myth is not your own story: not a story of your external life, not a story that explains the events of your life, not a story that holds together and has a beginning, a middle, and an end. The personal myth is not a story at all, though we might try to reach and express that myth by telling stories.

In order to distinguish more carefully between your own story and your personal myth, we might notice the interplay in culture between myth and mythology. In mythology, *mythos* and *logos* come together. *Logos* is the telling, or as Heidegger would say, the laying out, of the elements of the myth. *Logos* is the sewing together but not the tearing apart. Mythology weaves myth into story, though myth itself tends to unravel itself, like Penelope weaving and unraveling as the myth of Odysseus unfolds. Both movements in myth are necessary, though mythographers prefer to weave. Their fantasy, so different from the vase painters and cathedral artists, is to bring it all together. Robert Graves, Mircea Eliade, and Joseph Campbell all search for a unifying theme to tie myth together: the moon goddess, creation, or the heroic quest. Levi-Strauss himself makes fragments of myth, but these are rational pieces neatly sliced and brought into balance and contrast. When myth decays and fragments on its own, it creates confusion and wonder, not order and clarity. Picasso, in line with ancient artists who saw the myth within mythology, makes simple line drawings of scenes from Ovid, or places the mythic bull on the kaleidoscopic screen of his "Guernica" and other paintings.

In league with the tendency to unify myth, but even more dangerous, is the desire to canonize a mythology, to make it law. The story that carries deep, moving, stimulating generative, animating *images* of myth itself becomes codified, canonized, authoritatively interpreted, memorized, institutionalized, verified, historiographed, cartographied, concordanced, philologized, cross-referenced, theologized, philosophized, folklorized, sanctified, and ossified. A mythological orthodoxy arises that not only rejects all other mythological traditions, but also resists the natural tendency of myth to multiply itself, to fragment and offer self-contradiction and self-destruction. Where myth calls for a Platonic memory, a reminiscence of the figures and forms which inhabit and shape psychic space and time, orthodox mythology would be memorized by rote and quoted by verse. When you make such an effort to remember the mythology, you forget the myth.

It is also curious that an individual committed, as we say, to an orthodox mythology, will not admit the mythic nature of the object of his faith. Use the word "myth" in any intimate relation to a religious person's belief, and you are asking for a fight. A fixed mythology promises truth, while a myth offers a mere fable to help imagine events.

Myth is fluid, spontaneous, immediate, ephemeral. It emerges from a landscape and emanates from a person or situation. The function of mythology is not to provide us with myth, but to serve as an exemplar so we will know myth when it appears. But in our quest for myth, we often get confused and grasp at mythologies.

Mythology prepares us for the emergence of myth, as when a rosy-fingered dawn shows up on the horizon and we are reminded of Aurora of mythology, her connections with Aphrodite, and a sensual way of being in the world. If, remembering Aurora, we take notice of sensual and moving impressions of dawn that fill the lungs with airy sensations and set small fires in the heart, then dawn is in the psyche and is a figure of myth. But Aurora is not the myth.

When you meet the Buddha on the road, kill him. When you see Aurora in a Texas sky, kill her. It is not the Buddha one seeks, but the Buddha Nature, the Zen priests teach. It is not Aurora that makes the landscape mythic, but dawn itself known in her divinity.

Myth is fresh. Or, to use a word favored by the poet Wallace Stevens who was concerned about these things, myth is "dewy." In an often quoted passage from his poem "Asides on an Oboe," Stevens describes a fantasy I would think essential for a mythic sensibility:

> . . . *there is still*
> *The impossible possible philosophers' man,*
> *The man who has had the time to think enough,*
> *The central man, the human globe, responsive*
> *As a mirror with a voice, the man of glass,*
> *Who in a million diamonds sums us up.*
>
> *He is the transparence of the place in which*
> *He is and in his poems we find peace.*

I don't see this "man of glass" as "somebody," as a good poet or artist. I see him as a fantasy available to us all. The mythic sense of things comes when we ourselves are the man of glass, the transparence of the place. Myth is favored, too, when that beauty of dawn is taken in, made into a style of perception, when the world appears in the freshness of moist morning dew and one's imagination is wet with innocence, before the late afternoon world of Freud and Jung and D. H. Lawrence and the American Indian.

I would like to borrow a few more lines from Wallace Stevens where he calls for a "dewy" imaginal vision of things. When he speaks of poetry we can easily substitute myth. From "Notes Toward a Supreme Fiction":

> *The poem refreshes life so that we share,*
> *For a moment, the first idea . . . It satisfies*
> *Belief in an immaculate beginning*
>
> *And sends us, winged by an unconscious will,*
> *To an immaculate end.*

And then from "An Ordinary Evening in New Haven":

> *The poem is the cry of its occasion,*
> *Part of the res and not about it.*
> *The poet speaks the poem as it is,*
>
> *Not as it was: part of the reverberation*
> *Of a windy night as it is, when the marble statues*
> *Are like newspapers blown by the wind. He speaks*
>
> *By sight and insight as they are. There is no*
> *Tomorrow for him. The wind will have passed by,*
> *The statues will have gone back to be things about.*

Let me now be more plain in my talk about the personal myth. In answer to the question I posed at the beginning, I would say yes, the personal myth is a myth in every sense. We can speak of myth at the personal level, and like all myth, that myth is not true, as Jung implied, but it is animating.

The personal myth is not the story of your life. "Autobiography" is often defined as one's own (*auto*) writing (*graphe*) about the course of one's life (*bios*). I would rather say that autobiography, in the model Jung has given us which is in many ways mythic, is the differentiated life (*bios*) that writes (*graphe*) oneself (*auto*). A mythic autobiography would tell of the inner geography, the animals, the gods, and the unnatural events that come to the surface as a life. We get at this myth, not by telling the story of a life, but by telling its stories, over and over again, with all their many versions and contradictions. It is curious that once Jung presented the relatively mythic view of his *bios*, later biographers have all failed in their efforts. A biography of Jung now comes across like an expedition to find Noah's ark, or a recreation of Odysseus' likely route on the actual Mediterranean: the myth is swallowed up by mythology.

Mythic orthodoxy is also as much a problem in the personal myth as it is in culture. Just as an individual may well have trouble glimpsing *his* myth beyond the rigid orthodoxy of his childhood religious convictions, so he might have trouble seeing through the opaque story he has always told about himself: the story that explains why things are difficult now in the present. And, just as a person has difficulty seeing the mythic nature of his childhood religious convictions, so he has trouble seeing, as myth, his understandings of life, that story he calls an identity. Somewhere along the way, we become convinced of the *truth* of a particular life story: my father was too strict, I had an unhappy childhood, I was an unloved and unwanted child, and so on. These stories may trap the myth of a person's life like a bubble of air in a crystal ball. In pursuit of the truth, the myth is lost.

Jung's emphasis on *his own* story is important because the tendency is to borrow mythologies as we look for myth.

Culturally, we go to the East, or to Greece, or in America to the Indian. Personally, we read biographies, perhaps mythically—to find fragments of images for our reflection, but also likely to steal a truth, an insight, a solution to a problem, an identity: *imitatio Christi, imitatio Jungiana.* Could it be a reaction to this temptation to borrow a mythology that we turn to astrology where the emphasis is on the individual and his origins, founded upon the exact time and place of birth? Could it also be that the fascination with childhood as the source of maturity is a way of claiming our own stories, our own myth? It would be worth a lecture in itself to draw comparisons between mythologies of origin, creation stories, and personal stories of childhood. In an imaginal way, ontogeny recapitulates phylogeny, as the Freudians say. In his essay on "screen memories," those misleading memories that try to hide the frightening facts, Freud makes some remarks about childhood that are quite provocative when heard in the context of personal myth:

> *It may indeed be questioned whether we have any memories at all* from *our childhood: memories* relating to *our childhood may be all that we possess. Our childhood memories show us our earliest years not as they were but as they appeared at the later periods when the memories were revived. In these periods of revival, the childhood memories did not, as people are accustomed to say,* emerge; *they were formed at that time. And a number of motives, which had* no concern with historical accuracy *had their part in this forming them as well as in the selection of the memories themselves.*

A passage like this from Freud is usually quoted to demonstrate that it is not childhood traumas that make us neurotic, but rather our present thoughts about childhood. We may also be reminded by Freud's words that the misty eon of childhood is as unknown, as much a period of dream time to the individual as the once-upon-a-time past of a culture. Fantasies of childhood may well contribute much to our mythic sense. But these fantasies are often demythicized and taken as fixed, orthodox explanations of present problems. We even try to prove their historical accuracy. An old friend calls and says: "Do you remember when we were children? Did my parents make life difficult for me? Were they mean to me?" The quest for the historical childhood directs us away from the personal myth.

The personal myth parallels cultural mythology also in its relation to ritual. In culture, ritual is sometimes seen as the enactment of myth, sometimes as its source. The relation between myth and ritual in culture gives some clues as to ways the ego might deal with myth at the personal level.

On the negative side, we could notice how certain rituals in life perpetuate a rigid monolithic myth. Defensiveness, remaining stuck in feeling and in repeated patterns, insistence on control and understanding, maintaining rationalistic choices and following ideologies—all these might be ways of ritualizing an orthodox myth. The ego can, however, ritualize more effectively.

Dreams offer some clues on various roles the ego can play in relation to personal mythic figures. They sometimes show the ego acting as host, housing people of fantasy, introducing them to each other, learning their names, becoming acquainted with them, caring for their needs, listening to what they have to say. These *rituals of cordiality* could serve an important function in giving myth its place.

We all know that the dream-ego often merely watches the dream action and observes its personalities without becoming part of the action itself. Watching your mythic episodes unfold and its major and minor characters appear is like ritual theater—the observance of holy events given in the religious connotation of the word "observe."

We also know that culturally myth is an oral tradition in which not *the* story but *stories* are told and retold, with formula and variation. Telling the many stories of your life, telling dreams and secrets, ritually keep the myth alive. Such tellings serve no pragmatic function, but they do serve the psyche, especially when the stories are not linear, unified, and told as explanation. Stories keep the mythic figures, places, and events before our eyes. These figures may, of course, take the shape of friends and acquaintances from life and yet these people, like actors on a stage, may present the mythic figures for observation. As Jung says, "Other people are established inalienably in my memories only if their names were entered in the scrolls of my destiny from the beginning, so that encountering them was at the same time a kind of recollection."

I might say a word about dream and the personal myth, since Joseph Campbell has frequently written and remarked that dream is to the individual what myth is to a society; that is, that dream is personal myth. I would not emphasize the dream as a guide like mythology or as a kind of sacred scripture offering insight as a deep level. Rather I would point to the fragmented quality of dreams. Dreams are more like paintings—separate, individual, distinct, and not part of a whole—than they are a mythological system. We do not turn to dreams to find the personal myth, but rather to see elements of a mythic world that is not the dream itself. Turning dreams into mythology stands the same dangers as any kind of mythologizing: namely, the tendency to unify and codify, to find in them a source of truth and guidance rather than imagining.

I have said some things about myth but have so far paid little attention to the word "personal." It is a difficult word to talk about, and I have been content to allow the connotations of that word to suffice. But we can take the notion of "personal" somewhat deeper than usual by noticing an element common to its many etymological derivations. The word "person" is often related to the Greek *prosopon*, meaning "face." It is also connected to the Etruscan God Phersu, a masked figure who receives souls and accompanies them to the Underworld. He is a Hermes figure of sorts with the special attribute of the mask. His name is also related to Persephone.

In thinking about *face* and the personal myth, I want to avoid the temptation to see the face as a unifying factor. A face is not a mask. It is more like many masks, never static, usually expressive, a malleable form for the mythic movements behind it or within it. A person is many faces; we can say without contradiction that the face seen is a mask revealing the faces of myth. The personal myth is the collection of faces from the Underworld, and seeing your myth is being guided to that Underworld to observe its particulars. Perhaps then the myth behind the idea of a personal myth is not a story, not a familiar classical mythic tale, but simply the image of Phersu, the little-known masked god.

To be consistent with what has been said about myth, I would have to suggest that there is no single myth behind the idea of the personal myth. Another mythological fragment that serves at this time as a way of imagining the personal myth is the episode in the Odyssey that involves Kirke. According to this story, Odysseus and his men, having gone through various ordeals and having survived shipwreck, see Kirke's island and are fascinated. They are charmed by its circular nature ("Kirke" refers to the circling of a predatory animal) and the smoke that rises from its very center. This, for the Jungian, would be the mandala.

The men are taken in by this wonderful abstract shape. They are drawn to its center, they feel the pull of centripetal force. And they are turned into swine, utterance turned to grunts, nourished on slop, and penned in. Is this what the illusion of wholeness, centering, perfect geometries, and beauty does? Odysseus himself is cautious, and he is given some good advice by Hermes who happens to cross his path. Hermes tells him to make some show of attack. It does seem that you have to attack luring mythologies so as not to be penned in by them.

Odysseus is also given the plant *moly*, a legendary antidote to epilepsy, or uncontrolled manic acting out. You don't have to go wild over a myth. *Moly* also favors sleep, dreaming, and eros. It seems in our mythologies we have to let them be in our sleep; we have to continue to dream them and move where eros leads, not where truth and logos apparently reside.

Although Odysseus spends some happy time in the circle of Kirke and knows the pleasures of the mandala, eventually he has to move on, to the Underworld in fact, where he has to see some faces not in life. It could be that even for those of us deeply interested in myth, we have to do without the comfort of the perfectly formed, encircling cycle of stories called a mythology. Knowing something about mythology can be as much an obstacle as an aid to finding your myth.

With this emphasis in mind on the negative way into myth, I would like to conclude with a quotation from Samuel Beckett, who maintains the tension between the fullness and the emptiness of stories and words. He concludes his novel *The Unnameable* in this way:

> *I can't go on, you must go on, I'll go on, you must say words, as long as there are any, until they find me, until they say me, strange pain, strange sin, you*

must go on, perhaps it's done already, perhaps they have said me already, perhaps they have carried me to the threshold of my story, before the door that opens on my story, that would surprise me, if it opens, it will be I, it will be the silence, where I am, I don't know, I'll never know, in the silence you don't know, you must go on, I can't go on, I'll go on.

References

Freud, Sigmund. "Screen Memories" (1899). *Collected Papers.* Edited by James Strachey. London: The Hogarth Press, 1950, pp. 47–69.

Jung, C. G. *Memories, Dreams, Reflections.* Edited by Aniela Jaffe. Translated by Richard and Clara Winston. New York: Vintage Books, 1963.

Kerenyi, C. *Dionysos: Archetypal Image of Indestructible Life.* Translated by Ralph Manheim. Bollingen Series LXV.2. Princeton: Princeton University Press, 1976.

Olney, James. "Some Versions of Memory / Some Versions of Bios: The Ontology of Autobiography." *Autobiography: Essays Theoretical and Critical.* Edited by James Olney. Princeton: Princeton University Press, 1980.

Dream City Green

ONE OF SAMUEL Beckett's early characters, after whom a novel was named, is Watt, a man who embodies the essence of Beckett's vision. Beckett looks out of his expatriate French windows, far from the emerald isle of his birth, and sees a wasteland where there is no hope, no growth, no possibility of renewal. Watt, whose name suggests a thing rather than a person, seems to portray a facet of human consciousness utterly civilized, acquiescent to the wasteland, willing to live schizophrenically under the bomb. "And if there were two things that Watt loathed," says Beckett, "one was the earth, and the other was the sky."

It is tempting to slip into a one-sided view of things when we idealize the city as the place of human achievement and then imply or generate a devaluation of whatever is not city. A certain hubris colors our praise of the city so that an apparent conflict arises between the red brick, black streets, and gray concrete of the city's buildings and roads on the one hand, and nature's green on the other. The rugged backwoodsman-type romanticizes the forest and the farm, saying that green is what truly nourishes the soul. The city-slicker in turn romanticizes the polis and sets it up as the place where human culture reaches its zenith. For him the city wall of old or the modern expressway belt is a welcome border between rustic vulgarity and urban civility. For the city-born, the only gods are city gods. The words we use for godlessness betray our one-sided sense of divinity. A "pagan," from the Latin *paganus*, is a mere country villager, and "heathen" is someone who lives on the heath, far away from civilization.

Now what I want to do is to see if there is a way out of this schizoid polarity of city and wilderness. Obviously, individuals, city people, have the option of retreating into the woods, backpacking and hiking, getting some of nature's green into their hearts. But what about the city itself? Is there some way of finding a rapprochement between civic gray and natural green? The two are enemies at times. The city bulldozers tear up trees right and left, set up shallow-rooted condos where old oaks used to stand reaching deep into the earth and groping at the sky. On the other hand, as Phil Oaks, the folk singer from Detroit who died a dozen years ago, sang: "a blade of grass can break through any concrete city workers lay." Can there be, within the city, a reconciliation with green?

The split between culture and nature is a sign of a shallow appreciation of each. And when either is idealized and romanticized, we can be sure that neither is being lived very deeply. So the task is to deepen our sense of the city and of nature's green, and that means getting closer to the fantasy in each.

It is not unusual for the setting of a dream to be a city. Buildings are under construction and skyscrapers tower over the dream landscape. You find yourself walking down crowded streets, main thoroughfares, and dark alleys. You enter shops, houses, stores, or factories. You take an elevator, or you climb laboriously up a steep stairway. Traffic jams the streets, or you get lost on a misty deserted corner far away from the center of commerce. As with any dream image, it is impossible to say what these city locales mean, but it is important to remember that the city of dream is not identical with the actual city. The dream city is an image. It is a *psychological* topos—not an actual place but a place of imagination. The city that appears in a dream may have something to say about our *fantasy* of the actual city, but it may also reflect a city facet of the dreamer. The psyche has its city side—its culture, history, ethnicity, density, life-styles, economics, government, transportation, streets, perimeters, and parks. In a dream we may behold certain psychological avenues down which we promenade or roads along which we are driven—by impulse, compulsion, or fascination. The dream city may give some picture of psychological developments and construction under way. The dream city may map out districts and boroughs of the psyche's settlement. So let us keep in mind as we talk about parks, gardens, and lawns, mixing the actual green and imaginal green in a leafy salad of interpretation, that the real focus of our attention is dream city green.

Actual cities are greener than you might think. If you were to take a helicopter ride and fly over the city you would see large patches of green—the tree tops under which the city lay as under an immense umbrella. You would also see the green of parks and lawns and highway medians. If you were to walk the streets you would look up at the signs and find Oak Lawn, Highland Park, Park Lane, Forest Lane, Live Oak, Walnut Hill, Greenway Park, Greenville, Elm Street, Old City Park, Oak Cliff, and Timberlawn—all images of green. If you were to go to Texas Stadium or to the Cotton Bowl you would find yourself stunned by the brilliant green of the smooth, flat, sprawling astro-turf. Green, which we usually associate with nature, growth, springtime, summer, wilderness, and undeveloped land is in the city.

In general the color green represents nature's growth and renewal. Hope, we say, is green. It looks to the future with youthful optimism. Green is young, inexperienced, not yet jaundiced by hard reality. Green is untutored and naive. The green traffic light speaks a youthful language: all go and no inhibition. Give us the green light, and we'll try anything. There is an illness that was traditionally called the "green sickness," or more officially, "chlorosis." It strikes women and is manifested, says the Oxford English Dictionary, as "curiosity for novelty rather than sound truth." And to be "green-in-the-eye" is to be gullible, again not hindered by reason, realism, or relevance. Green is springtime, with new shoots and buds, with fresh expectation and inspiring renewal.

But not all that is green is so charming. Green often appears as the color opposite the vital and vigorous red of human blood. Green ooze in humans or in insects recently squashed is revolting. Novelty shops sell little green garbage cans filled with a sticky substance intended to nauseate, in fun of course, called "Green Slime." Another of Beckett's characters, in the novel *Mercier and Camier*, cannot stand green. Beckett says of him: "Whenever he saw green he turned red." Anyone devoted to the black side of experience might be expected to be embarrassed by human potential green. Zombies tend to be greenish, as do The Hulk, E.T., The Thing, Frankenstein, and the Jolly Green Giant. It is also commonly assumed that when we are finally visited by

people from outer space, they will be "little green men."
There is something alien to human life in green creatures.

This notion that green is alien to human life is a major factor in psychological green. The mythology of Artemis portrays her cruelty and her untouchability. When the hunter Orion is running beside her he accidentally touches her jacket, and she sends a scorpion after him to kill him. She turns Actaion into a stag to be torn to bits by his dogs, only because he spied upon her naked at her bath. Nature will not be approached by human eyes or skin without turning cold and dangerous. Green nature is alien. John Fowles in *The Tree* talks about "Green Man" and, citing Richard Jeffries, depicts the green wild as

> the ultra-humanity of all that is not man . . . not with us or against us, but outside and beyond us, truly alien. It may sound paradoxical, but we shall not cease to be alienated—by our knowledge, by our greed, by our vanity—from nature until we grant it its unconscious alienation from us." (n.p.)

The psyche, too, is green in that it is alien, not human, resisting control by human will and designs, not to be humanized and "developed" but allowed its alien status, its own quirks and purposes, its "ultra-humanity."

The easiest answer to the question about the nature of green in dreams is Artemis, who is clearly wild nature herself: the dark, not altogether trustworthy, hazy green of the deep forest and the bright green of beans, peas, and ivy. She is the translucent green of Redwood forest ferns and the green of ocean-fields of unripe wheat. Artemis green in a dream seems to speak to the virginal space of the soul, where unformed, delicate, vegetative fantasy and feeling romp and roam. An ancient ritual performed in honor of Artemis was known as the Dance of the Plants in which dancers circled the dancing ground with plants on their heads. They were vegetables animated by Artemis, showing that anima itself is vegetative, plantlike, and green.

Plants are occasionally prominent in dreams, suggesting what the medieval philosophers referred to as the "vegetative soul." The plant psyche would be those unformed, unmoving, yet living green psychic realities beyond reason and beyond self-movement. They might be utterly inchoate, primitive, beautiful to look at and to touch, thriving on their own or demanding great care (household plants of the psyche). They may appear in life as phenomena of the body, as vegetable: rashes, blushes, aches, growths, pains, and pleasures. They are truly psychic, but they are not human. They are alien to consciousness of a rational sort. Artemis appears as the atmosphere of the woods, the air in all that is natural, overgrown, spontaneously germinated.

The city is not complete without Artemis, without the pristine qualities of her virginal nature in the green of Central Park, Golden State Park, or White Rock Lake. The city, usually given over to business and the demands of civil survival, is made polytheistic by the presence of Artemis with her parks and gardens. Statues of Diana dominate in famous formal gardens in Britain and in Europe, indicating that the Artemesian spirit in a civilized green place has been widely recognized and acknowledged.

But is Artemis *the* Green Goddess? Pictures on salad dressing labels don't reveal the identity of this goddess. Maybe she is the nature spirit Chloris, who appears in Botticelli's *Primavera* as the first pale-green hue of springtime. Chloris is the green in chlorophyll, chloroform, and Clorets. Fresh breath is green, too.

Green is also the color of Venus, *the* goddess of the garden
at Rome. Green is plush, pleasant, opulent, and sensual. The
great gardens of Renaissance English manors often had a
statue of Venus at the heart of their labyrinths. The green
hedges shaped into the forms of animals and the low bushy
mazes were understood as artful taming of nature, but they
were also the natural place for lovers, and statues of Eros and
Venus looked down on those strolling children of the sensual
goddess. Therefore, taking the formal gardens as a guide we
may expect to find the spirit of Venus, with all her sensuality
and body, in dream city green. But the relationship between
Venus, Diana, and the imaginal city is subtle and compli-
cated and demands some sorting out.

Of all the many literary sources that offer a path into this
green theology of the dream city, none is more appropriately
complex and engaging than the medieval story of *Sir Gawain
and the Green Knight*. This fourteenth-century anonymous
tale suggests some curious things about the conflict between
nature and culture. It is New Year's Day at King Arthur's
court, celebrated in grand style. In rides a knight all dressed
in green, his hair and complexion green, his horse green, the
axe in his hand of green-hammered gold—"graven in green
with graceful designs." The Green Knight challenges anyone
present to strike him a blow with the axe, provided he can
give a return blow in exactly a year. Sir Gawain takes up the
axe and slices off the visitor's head. But this doesn't hinder
the Green Knight, who tells Gawain to meet him a year later
at the Green Chapel. Ten months later Gawain goes off in
search of the Green Chapel and stops at a castle along the
way. The lord of this castle, Bertilak, is gracious and provides
him a place to rest, and when he goes off on daily hunts he
asks Gawain to stay behind and be entertained by his wife.
Bertilak first hunts a deer, than a boar, and finally a fox. He

makes a deal with Gawain, that they will give each other
something of what each has acquired during the day. While
the lord is at the hunt, his wife attempts to seduce Gawain,
but she fails, except to get a modest kiss. When the lord
returns home from the hunt, he gives Gawain a portion of
the game, and Gawain greets him with a kiss. He does this
twice, but on the third day, when she realizes she can't
seduce Gawain, the wife gives him the green cincture she
wears around her waist, which she says will protect him. This
time Gawain breaks his promise and does not tell the hus-
band about the gift of the green cincture.

Gawain wraps the green silk around his waist and goes to
the Green Chapel, which turns out to be a mound of earth,
all overgrown, the "most evil holy place" Gawain had ever
seen. The Green Knight appears, and Gawain offers his head
to the axe. At the first blow he twitches, revealing a strain of
cowardice unfitting in a knight of the Round Table. At the
next blow he doesn't move; the axe falls and nicks his neck,
sending forth a few drops of blood. Then the Green Knight
reveals himself to be Bertilak, lord of the castle. He had de-
vised the entire test himself and knew of the protective girdle.
He admits that the venture was a test of virtue, and that Gawain has failed for love of his own life. But he absolves Gawain of his fault and offers him the green cincture as a gift.
"Seeing it is as green as my gown," he says, "you may think
about this trial when you throng in company with paragons
of princes."

Like so many traditional stories, this tale seems to be a por-
trayal of an initiation, in this case initiation into green. As in
typical religious initiations around the world, there is the
ritual of death, the pouring out of blood, the confrontation
with a new order, and the ordeal or test. But this is a particularly subtle story for Gawain is humbled, brought down

from the hubris of the Round Table where cultivation and perfectly controlled behavior are the norm. He is finally shown to have human blood; he is not just a spiritual paragon. He learns through his failure, through his fall. Gawain arrives at a crisis of decision when he fails to live up to the agreement with Bertilak. He fails his accustomed virtue, but that failure turns out to be his salvation. Through it he walks into the world of green, formerly wild beyond measure, thus recalling the "wild man" in medieval thought and imagination who was identified with Satan, so uncivil and lacking in standard virtue was he.

The modern city is not unlike King Arthur's Round Table, and, to be less literal, the dream city itself as a metaphor for a facet of psychological life may betray an Arthurian predilection for high culture, manners, and formality. In themselves there is nothing wrong with these manners, but they tend to constellate an overpowering response from the green wild. As all the medievalists who comment on the story of Sir Gawain point out, the Green Man is a traditional and widely acknowledged figure of untamed nature. Pubs in England, so many of these scholars remind us, are named after this "Green Man," as though the place where repressions are lifted and where pleasure takes precedence over manners is his shrine.

In the modern city where green is not given its due, and in the modern psyche where green is considered a mere border of little importance, the Green Knight may appear in all his frightening power to threaten, but also to heal by ordeal. There is an image of homeopathic therapy in this story of the Green Knight who arranges to have a belt of green wrapped around Sir Gawain in order to protect him as he learns the power of green. Green protects against green. And in this particular case, it is the green of Venus. The cincture of

Aphrodite was known to have magical power; so the green cord around Sir Bertilak's wife, the priestess of love, had the power to deal with wild green. This motif suggests that a Venusian sensuality, in fact an appreciation and cultivation of all the moist, green spirits of Venus might protect us from wild nature, from the natural wild and from the wildness that erupts from within. It's a subtle point: not Artemis but Venus offers a way to deal with the threatening upheavals of our wild nature. Not literal sexuality—a mistake often made in modern life, unlike the story of Sir Gawain—but a putting on of the Venusian in the region of our loins, becoming green in fantasy. The green of sexuality is what is redemptive and salvific in the face of raging nature.

The Garden

One way a city can put on Venus' green near her loins is to cultivate gardens. A psychological study of gardens, covering its vast history and intricate subtlety, would help us understand in detail what we might gain from honoring green in the city. We could appreciate the psychological richness of the garden, for instance, by wandering with Gilgamesh in the garden of the Gods:

> In this immortal garden stands the Tree
> With trunk of gold, and beautiful to see.
> Beside a sacred fount the tree is placed,
> With emeralds and unknown gems is graced.
> (Moynihan, *Epic of Gilgamash*)

Other emerald cities come to mind as well—such as Oz and the heavenly city of Revelations, both images of fulfillment of utter beauty. And there is the famous garden of Eden, of course, called Paradise, a name brought by Xenophon in 401 B. C. from Persia, where he was a professional soldier and where he saw magnificent gardens. In the Judeo-Christian imagination, creation is a garden; human life originates in a garden, and consciousness expels us from the garden, now guarded by an angel. To get back into this garden we may have to go through the angel, through an angelic sense of things, through figures and spirits that are not human and not divine, through an intense fantasy that is as close to nature as are the spirits and daimons. We know today that gardens are a place for recreation, but with the Persian word for garden in mind—Paradise or *pairidaeza*—we can understand the garden's green as a place of re-creation. So green fantasy is renewal in quite a profound sense: it is a return to paradise, a sense of creation as archetypal, always accessible except to consciousness and moral judgment (the tree of the knowledge of good and evil). To cultivate green is to be always in the place of creativity, to be in Eden naming the animals and exploring the world. We need not moralize against Paradise as though to go there is to return to childhood (Freud) or to regress to a deadening uroboric state of being (Neumann). The green garden has its place, so that renewal, creativity, childhood, and closeness with both divinity and animal life need not be taken literally. To literalize this garden in a romantic fantasy of creativity and pollyanna is to overlook the very nature of gardens as places of fantasy and imagination.

In his famous poem "Fern Hill," Dylan Thomas rhythmically orchestrates a child's vision of green days under a green sun. But we must not get caught in the literalism of childhood when reading this poem, because the subtle poet depicts not only actual childhood but a permanent greenness, with a darker shade of green toward the end.

Medieval and Renaissance gardens were places of studied imagination. They took their inspiration from Pliny whose own garden shows the variety of fantasy a garden affords. His garden had in it a terrace, a lawn, shrubs shaped like animals, dwarf trees, a hippodrome, an open lawn shaped into a half-circle at one end, a ring of trees covered in ivy, a little meadow and apple trees—and for Artemis, a wild section full of the "careless beauties of nature." The garden of the Medici in Florence was inspired by the work of the architect Alberti, but it was also influenced by the philosophy of Marsilio Ficino who believed that a person's environment should be thoroughly cultivated as a place of images which infuse the person with a wide variety of spirits. A contemporary of Ficino, Francesco Colonna, published a book, *Hypnerotomachia Poliphili*, a description of the dream journey of Polyphilo, who finds himself in luxurious gardens such as the island of Cythera, home of Aphrodite, the entire space of which is a garden focused around a tree sacred to Venus (Strong, 17). An illustration in this book shows lovers sitting and walking together in the garden, making music, picking flowers, and enjoying each other. Here is a precise image of dream city green emphasizing the Venusian spirit.

But other spirits were present. Renaissance gardens were sometimes provided with dark shaded groves, blackened hues of green predominating, where one could go to nurse one's melancholy humor. Portraits show young men dressed in black, wearing large floppy hats (a typical accent in depictions of Saturn), sitting on lawns darkened by overarching trees. They are in typical melancholy pose, their heads in their hands. The title page of Robert Burton's *Anatomy of Melancholy* pictures a philosopher, head in hand, under the shade of a green leafy tree set apart from the geometric formal garden.

A garden, therefore, is a polytheistic space itself, where formally one might encounter the spirits of Artemis, Venus, Saturn, and one I have not mentioned—Priapus. Priapus, the phallic god who is an embarrassment to anyone who would make divinity ever proper and bodiless, stands in the garden, short, fat, erect, obscene—a scarecrow that would keep all those pure airy bird-like spirits away from his private retreat. In the city of dream the garden is a place of fantasy, where nature is turned into imaginal creatures, like hedges sheared into the shapes of animals. It is also a labyrinth, a maze where one enters deep into the interior of life, giving the secretary of interior a serious charge indeed. According to the Renaissance theory of gardens, nature is tamed there, but for us it is more the case that nature is made imaginative and imaginal. Paradoxically a garden requires a sophisticated knowledge of nature, knowing her varieties and laws, in order to effect an *opus contra naturam*, a work against nature in favor of fantasy.

Etymologically a garden is a walled space, a place set apart from the world of city functions. It is a place where birds can take their baths and lovers share their secrets. In Slavic languages, in fact, a garden is a city insofar as the word *gradu*, related to our word "garden," means both city and garden, as in Leningrad. It is also related to our word "yard." This etymology leads to the last aspect of green I want to consider, the image of a green space set apart from the rest of the city, open like a lawn, and protected by its borders. This will lead us to imagine green as something even less literal than a garden, a place where imagination can let loose.

The Village Green and Billiards

What is peculiar about a lawn besides the fact that it is green? A lawn, unlike a garden, is a green patch of land, generally unobstructed. In fact, the beauty of a lawn is its uselessness and its lack of encumberances. It is a piece of green emptiness in an otherwise cluttered world and in that regard is not unrelated perhaps to the Zen garden, the main portion of which is empty, raked sand. The lawn, the park, the village green—what is remarkable about these pieces of land is their emptiness. They are the *field* where imagination can go to work without limitation except for the borders around the green, its *temenos*. The city green, therefore, is a place to do anything that is not pragmatic or important. So dream city green is that place in the psyche that is an open field: the place for play, for conversation, for solitary meditation, for simply looking and sensing. It is a place where the wind becomes noticeable, or psychologically where spirits can blow and be perceived.

Lawn tennis and especially lawn bowling, on the bowling green, make it clearer what this village or city green is. It is the field—in the extended sense of that word—where imaginative play happens, and therefore it is an extremely important parcel of land. There we reflect on the patterns of all that goes on outside the borders of the green. We play games like Boccie, Pall-Mall, croquet, bowling, golf, tennis—games that call to mind the moving forces at work in life that is not pure green. We toss in our ball and see if we can move without colliding into hazards and obstacles, including other balls.

Bowling as a metaphor for life is not a new idea. Nicolas of Cusa wrote a theological treatise, *De Ludo Globi*, (*The Ball Game*), with the same idea in mind. Cusanus had a profound sense of religion as something much deeper than the creeds and rites and traditions of any one culture. He uses an ordinary ball game as a metaphor for that religious life, suggesting that practice makes a better player:

We learn to know that these inclinations and natural curvings are made straight by virtuous practice so that at last after many variations and unstable circlings and curvings we come to rest in the kingdom of life. For you see that one person throws the ball in one way, another in another, with the same curve remaining in the ball. . . . The ball, having a heavy body and inclined towards the flat earth, is somewhat similar to the earthly condition of man, and its movement, because it is thrown by man, is somewhat similar to man's earthly pilgrimage.

We know that Egyptian games, among many others, were played to chart the fate of the soul. Francis Quarles, in the seventeenth century, published a book of emblems that went through many editions, portraying the drama of the soul in the imagery of gardens. One of these emblems depicts a bowling green in which Cupid, Mammon, and Satan play with "sinful thoughts" as the balls. Psychologically, then, green is the field in imagination where the balls are tossed and the fate of the soul is decided.

In this respect the green cloth on a billiard table is particularly interesting. Clearly it is an indoor version of lawn bowling or some similar game, and the green of the lawn is retained. In *The Compleat Gamester*, a book on games published first in 1710, there is an illustration on the frontispiece showing two men playing on a billiard table with rather crooked cues. An explanation in verse is appended and begins:

Billiards from Spain at first deriv'd its Name,
Both an ingenious, and a cleanly Game.
One Gamester leads (the Table green as Grass)
And each like Warriers strive to gain the Pass,
But in the contest e'er the Pass be won,

> Hazzards are many into which they run.
> Thus while we play on this Terrestrial Stage,
> Nothing but Hazzard doth attend each age.

Green here is the terrestrial stage on which we encounter hazards in our play. In an essay in *The Spectator*, a magazine published in London in the early years of the eighteenth century, Addison and Steele, essayists, chide students of their time for their playful, green tendencies to waste time. "Our younger students," they write, "are content to carry their speculations as yet no farther than bowling-greens, billiard tables, and such like places."

So the city green, or the billiard table, is useless, and yet it is the world, cleared of cultivated debris, upon which the game of life is played. The idea is developed much more subtly and beautifully by William Blake in his poem "The Echoing Green." This poem brings to a pitch the point I am trying to make about green, moving it farther from literalism and more into the soul.

> The sun does rise,
> And make happy the skies;
> The merry bells ring
> To welcome the Spring;
> The skylark and thrush,
> The birds of the bush,
> Sing louder around
> To the bells' cheerful sound,
> While our sports shall be seen
> On the Echoing Green.
>
> Old John, with white hair,
> Does laugh away care,
> Sitting under the oak,
> Among the old folk.
> They laugh at our play,
> And soon they all say:

"Such, such were the joys
When we all, girls and boys,
In our youth time were seen
On the Echoing Green."

Till the little ones, weary,
No more can be merry;
The sun does descend,
And our sports have an end.
Round the laps of their mothers
Many sisters and brothers,
Like birds in their nest,
Are ready for rest,
And sport no more seen
On the darkening Green.

In Blake's simple poem we see the city green as the place where life is remembered and where it is played. On the green, where there is no business of culture-building or life-making, generations come to make their reflections. Suzanne Langer discusses this poem in *Feeling and Form*, where she notes in particular the echoes: the play of children echoed in the memories of the old folk, again echoed in the birds in their nest. But I am interested in the echoes of green itself. The green lawn echoes a green of the soul, an essential, open, empty, bounded field. Birth, play, and death take place on this green, because about all three of these things we *are* green: inexpert and unpracticed.

To summarize: A person dreams of playing in a large city park, or walking with a lover in a lush garden, of cutting the grass on a sprawling lawn, of playing a game of snooker in a dimly lighted pool hall. This is Cusa's game, it is Venus's bower, it is Artemis's retreat, it is the hideaway of Priapus, it is Saturn's nook. If this green religion is honored, if green in its dappled meanings is in the imagination, if we see how important croquet of the soul is, then we may cease doing what

Joni Mitchell complains about: "pave paradise, put up a parking lot." We may also end the schizophrenia of romanticized city and romanticized wilderness.

To dream forward the city's green is to regain touch with our vegetative soul, our own soil and demands of climate and humidity. It is to cushion our loyalties to the senex King Arthur and feel again what it is like to be green. It is to recover many of those gods of the garden who prefer not to appear on the city streets. The greening of the city is a further discovery of its nature, while the greening of the soul's city opens up crowded space for the pleasures of sport and idle thought.

References

Fowles, John, and Horvat Frank. *The Tree*. Boston, Toronto: Little, Brown and Co., 1979.

Langer, Suzanne K. *Feeling and Form: A Theory of Art*. New York: Charles Schribner's Sons, 1953.

Strong, Roy. *The Renaissance Garden in England*. London: Thames and Hudson, 1979.

Watts, Pauline Moffitt. *Nicolaus Cusanus: A Fifteenth-Century Vision of Man*. Leiden: E. J. Brill, 1982.

Ficinian Psychology

In the year 1462 Cosimo de' Medici, powerful patriarch of the most influential family in Florence, made a gift of a piece of property to a dwarfish, lisping melancholic scholarly man, Marsilio Ficino. Cosimo presented a villa where the scholar could translate Plato, the Neoplatonists, and other authors to his heart's content. Ficino was the son of a physician, and his mother apparently was something of a psychic. Ficino took the position and not only translated whatever Cosimo wanted of antique literature, he also established Careggi, the villa, as a center of study, psychotherapy, astrological advice, music, and the revivification of the Platonic Academy.

The very notion of a Renaissance Psychology and accompanying therapy may seem strange to modern sophisticates who find the past remote, uninformed, and at the practical level, irrelevant. But Ficino cannot be dismissed so easily. Although he is generally known, if at all, as a theologian or Platonic philosopher, he was also a psychotherapist. His writings indicate that he was deeply concerned about the psyche or soul of the individual as well as the soul of his society. So his work constitutes a Renaissance kind of cultural psychology. He offers much advice about the practice of what we would call psychotherapy. He even provides a detailed description of his practice of music therapy.

But what is particularly important about Ficino, both as a figure in history and as an author we might regard seriously for our own benefit, is that he made intimate connections between psychology, art, and religion. After a long period of depression, he became a priest, and he was careful about what he said regarding occult matters. But his theories about the soul and its relation to life-style tie psychopathology closely to the art of life as well as to the life of art.

One of Ficino's most remarkable writings is his *Book of Life*. This is a three-volume work written mainly for scholars. Ficino was concerned about the sufferings of scholars—something he knew firsthand. So in these volumes he develops a theory of psychology, and particularly in the last volume he offers a host of practical remedies for psychological affliction. Volume three of the work is entitled: how life should be arranged according to the heavens. A glance at the book reveals that the "heavens" he is talking about is the astrological zodiac. Ficino adapts traditional astrology to his own reading of Platonic and Neoplatonic Philosophy. To this solid scholarly base, he mixes in some medieval medical practice, the occult reflections of the Hermetic tradition, and some family recipes. He admits as much himself when in the prologue to this last volume he writes: "our laboratory here, our antidotes, drugs, poultices, ointments and remedies, offer different things to different types of people."

Frances Yates helped make this practical side of Ficino's work more widely known in her book on Giordano Bruno. She truly captures the spirit of Ficino, the psychotherapist, and perhaps she suggests more than she intended to say when she describes the third volume of *The Book of Life*: "We might be in the consulting room of a rather expensive psychiatrist who knows that his patients can afford plenty of gold and holidays in the country, and flowers out of season." Yates talks about Ficino's work with images as "natural magic," not a bad description if the hocus-pocus is taken out of the idea of magic. An imagistic, culture-conscious, psychotherapy might be a more accurate, if burdensome, way to put it.

Nevertheless, Ficino's "natural magic"—with the emphasis on "natural"—is the core of his psychotherapeutic approach. Using the language Ficino adopts in *The Book of Life*, we can summarize the relationship between psyche and culture. The planets, he says, each hold a certain kind of "spirit." All these varieties of spirit are necessary nourishment for the soul, and therefore it is good practice to get as much of this spirit, and as much of its variety, as possible. The trick is to know which things in the world contain in them these different kinds of spirit. According to Ficino, things naturally "absorb" rays from the planets. So, a person can acquire a particular kind of spirit, and in greater or lesser quantity, by exposing himself to those things that are rich in that spirit. Not only natural things, but man-made things can also absorb the various spirits of the planets, provided they are made well with a sensitivity to the qualities of the individual planets.

Frances Yates makes the provocative suggestion that Botticelli's Primavera was felt, at least by some of Ficino's contemporaries, to be not a mere painting but an actual talisman, an effective source of the spirit of Venus. Botticelli, like so many artists during and after Ficino's lifetime, was deeply influenced by Ficino's theory of soul and culture. In

The Book of Life Ficino makes countless recommendations for making images or performing ritual actions that will draw forth the spirit of the planet desired. He also describes certain qualities and objects that are talismanic to the various planets and tells the dangers as well as the blessings each planet affords.

Before trying to express this archaic-sounding theory of psychology in modern terms, it will be necessary to look more closely at Ficino's notion of the soul. In chapter one of the third volume of *The Book of Life*, he presents the core of his theory in language that is dense and difficult yet nevertheless indicates how important soul is in his thought; for example, the chapter begins:

> If there were only intellect and body in the world, but no soul, the intellect would not be drawn to the body (for it is altogether immobile, and lacks the affect of motion, as if it were the furthest possible distance from the body), nor would the body be drawn to the intellect, since it is ineffective and inept in itself for such motion, and very remote from the intellect. So if a soul, conforming to each, is placed between them, each one is easily attracted to the other.

Ficino makes the soul an intermediary between mind and body. Without soul, body has no sense, no rationality of any kind, while without soul the mind is disembodied, cut off from the physical world. There are obviously profound theoretical issues involved in this description, but even on an ordinary level Ficino's point is valid. Without soul, perhaps without a sensitivity to depth, interiority, value, and reverberations of meaning, our ideas remain in our heads, our philosophers theorize without much impact on ordinary life, the body itself is neglected in favor of mind, we are caught in materialism and literalism without end, and there is gnawing sense that the soul has gone out of life. What Ficino describes is a kind of schizoid situation: mind and body split in a polarization that is to the detriment of the individual and of the culture.

Ficino goes on to speak of the *anima mundi*, or the soul of the world. The world, he says, is an animal. It is an organism in itself. Everything has its own unique "ratio"—we might say "character"—that corresponds to that character in the world soul. But things can lose their soulfulness. "There is nothing in the whole living world so deformed as that which has no soul, no gift of soul contained in it," says Ficino. So the purpose of the "physician of the soul" is to find those things rich in a variety of spirit so that using them the soul will be nourished.

This theory is quite abstract and intricate, but Ficino does provide some practical examples. Scholars, he says, are particularly susceptible to the depressions of Saturn. In their remote retreats and studies they are tempting the black, leaden character of Saturn. They have two choices of remedy in case they fall victim to Saturn: they can turn to an alternative, more benign spirit, like Venus or Jupiter. Ficino specifically recommends that scholars wear white clothes, following the practice of the Pythagoreans, in order to counter the blackness of Saturn. But the other alternative, the only truly effective and final way to deal with a saturnine pathology is to endure Saturn to the hilt. No band-aids of venusian or jovial spirit will finally work against this oppressive planetary "influence," but Saturn has his gifts to offer in spite of the suffering he brings. (Panofsky, Klibansky, and Saxl have sketched the history of this beneficence of Saturn in their splendid book *Saturn and Melancholy*.)

Ficino's constant reference to the planets, indeed his astrological thought in itself, suggests, if not taken too literally, that individual and social life has deep roots and is a mix of eternal factors that need to be felt vividly if life is to be more that superficial, if it is to have soul. Venus's sensuality and pleasure, Mars' sense of power and resourcefulness, Luna's rhythms and changeability—these and other deep patterns call for acknowledgment and respect. A culture or an individual life built on reason or the limited capacities and vision of ego-consciousness is cut off from its motivating power and profound sources of meaning and significance.

Ficino's theory of the planets and his concrete remedies for dealing with their absence or pathologizing oppression suggests two ways of living psychologically or soulfully. The first may be called "cultivation," the other "constellation" or "tempering." It is not enough to understand the causes or the historical roots of our individual and social problems. A psychological life calls for a cultivation of images. Ficino says directly that the makers of images know the various "planetary" qualities in the things of the world. We can cultivate a life in which actions are seen in relation to the deeper issues that give life its value and meaning. Action then is not merely literal, it has a ritual quality to it; that is to say, it speaks to the soul and nourishes the soul by attracting different kinds of spirit. Ficino's actual suggestions for this kind of life are quite concrete and almost simplistic. For example, a person in need of solar spirit—someone who needs more brightness in life and spirituality in general—should walk in open places where the sun can pour down on him. A less literal way of saying the same thing is to suggest that a person dispirited and dull might seek out people and places rich in the spirit he is lacking. Ficino recommends splashing a little wine on the temples when the spirit of Dionysus is prescribed. Exposure to the needed spirit is the point. Things are not only important to the body, they also affect the soul, whether nourishing it or depriving it of what it needs.

The cultivation of soul in life, then, is a central notion in Ficinian Psychology. It is a cultural psychology in the sense that one "makes soul" by cultivating it in the most ordinary contexts. Whether we are seeking a particular kind of spirit or not, the culture will provide its own varieties of spirit, complete with excess and poverty of various kinds of spirit. An ugly place, built only for utilitarian purposes, will convey that negative quality of spirit. Ficino was especially interested in architecture as a source of varieties of spirit. A building clearly has a unique spirit. But if a building is imageless, it lacks that vital talismanic quality, in the Ficinian sense, that is so important to soul. If no god is evoked, no spirit will be forthcoming. The soul suffers. Some buildings are quite functional (body) and others are intellectually fascinating (mind), but only the building made with intense images will attract the spirits so needed by the soul.

In *The Book of Life* the root metaphor for Ficino's psychology is astrology, more specifically the planets. To this astrological imagery he adds, as tradition had done for centuries earlier, the imagery of music. A person with all the planets at play in his psychological life would be an individual of good temperament. These planets, like the notes in a musical scale, have to be "tempered." They have to be "tuned in," so they sound clearly in the life and character of the person. The psyche for Ficino, then, is polycentric, at least when it is in good condition. As Ficino says, if you are ever faced with a choice among the planets, choose all of them.

Ficinian therapy, therefore, involves a diagnosis of the archetypal configuration of the psyche, and then some tempering of the soul, a cultivation of life so that the soul is "tuned." Tempering is an indirect process. It cannot be simple doctoring by the ego—filling in blank spaces with a dose of some missing planetary spirit. The method is to fill the environment with images that serve the polycentric psyche. In passing, Ficino recommends other ways to make sure the soul is tempered. If, for example, a troublesome bout with some malignant spirit afflicts the soul, the only thing to do might be to remain in the suffering, to feel as deeply as possible the tension created by this onslaught of an unfamiliar and unwanted spirit. Another way might be to follow the example of Ficino's pupil, Botticelli, and see the planets as seasonal. The Primavera shows the roles of Venus and Mercury in Spring. But the soul has its seasons, what Ficino himself might call the soul's lunar nature. There are times of increase, times of emptying or kenosis. There is youth, maturity, and old age. These need not be taken literally only, they might also refer to the aging of a quality of soul.

In addition to the emphasis on polycentricism in the psyche, Ficino also stresses the importance for each individual—we might also say each city and country—to discover its own dominant planet, its own guiding and perplexing daimon. It could be the dominant planet in one's birthchart, to use Ficino's image. Or it could be that peculiar complex that keeps appearing and interfering in life. One's daimon is both demon and angel, the source of talent, creativity, soul-making, and the source of pain and trouble. The point is to grapple with the daimon, perhaps for a lifetime, in order to allow its influence to permeate one's character and activity.

To summarize: Ficinian Psychology is expressed in occult language, but if that language is read metaphorically, it suggests a relationship between culture and the individual in which the individual's task is to make of culture a theater of images, while the psychological role of culture is to feed the soul with the spirit of those images. The psychotherapist, in this approach, is someone who, like Ficino, can read a person's life and environment for the images and varieties of spirit it contains. A modern Ficinian psychotherapist might have his or her own favorite image-systems and know imagery intimately in order to get a sense of the deeper spirits at work in an individual's life. The therapist would also have an interest in the individual's own private and familial "culture" and the image-life of the society. It is no accident that Ficino's theories generated excitement among artists and poets; he gave them a purpose. He placed their work at the heart of individual and social life. We might take that phenomenon—the astonishing artistic creativity of the Renaissance—to heart as a sign that psychology, art, and culture go together. The psychologist, at least the Ficinian kind, is concerned with soul wherever it appears. The psyche is to be found in art, in society, and in the individual's problems.

The Ficinian psychotherapist encourages a "cultivation" of soul in life. The therapist recognizes that the most ordinary things—for Ficino splashing wine on the temples, for a modern running through the park—is inseparable from the experience of the soul. Actions are rituals, insofar as they have soul-value. Language is myth, insofar as it speaks the themes of the psyche. The job of the psychologist is to help name the daimon, the ruling fantasy, the dominant note of fate, and to move toward its fulfillment. The cultural psychologist in particular can discover which spirits are at work affecting the soul of a city or a nation, and he can go about the difficult task of recommending a temperament of spirit rich in variety and deep in quality.

References

Ficino, Marsilio. *The Book of Life*. Translated by Charles Boer. Irving, Tex.: Spring Publications, 1980.

Kristeller, Paul Oskar. *The Philosophy of Marsilio Ficino*. Translated by Virginia Connant. Gloucester, Mass.: Peter Smith, 1964.

Moore, Thomas. *The Planets Within: Marsilio Ficino's Astrological Psychology*. Lewisburg, Pa.: Bucknell University Press, 1982.

Yates, Frances. *Giordano Bruno and the Hermetic Tradition*. New York: Vintage Books, 1964.